BLAZERS

TOP 10
UNEXPLAINED

TOP 10 ANCIENT MYSTERIES

by Lori Polydoros

Reading Consultant:
Barbara J. Fox
Reading Specialist
Professor Emerita
North Carolina State University

CAPSTONE PRESS
a capstone imprint

Blazers is published by Capstone Press,
1710 Roe Crest Drive, North Mankato, Minnesota 56003.
www.capstonepub.com

Library of Congress Cataloging-in-Publication Data
Polydoros, Lori, 1968–
Top 10 ancient mysteries / by Lori Polydoros.
p. cm. — (Blazers. Top 10 unexplained)
Summary: "Describes various ancient mysteries in a top-ten format"—Provided by publisher.
Includes bibliographical references and index.
ISBN 978-1-4296-8437-8 (library binding)
ISBN 978-1-62065-207-7 (ebook PDF)
1. Civilization, Ancient—Juvenile literature. 2. Curiosities and wonders—Juvenile literature. I.
Title. II. Title: Top ten ancient mysteries.
CB311.P65 2013
930—dc23
2012000116

Editorial Credits
Mandy Robbins, editor; Sarah Bennett, designer; Eric Gohl, media researcher;
    Laura Manthe, production specialist

Photo Credits
akg-images/Johann Brandstetter, 17
Alamy/Bailey-Cooper Photography, 19 (back); Barry Iverson, 15; JTB Photo
    Communications, Inc., 11
Bridgeman Art Library/Look and Learn, 5
Corbis/PoodlesRock, 9; Science Faction/Norbert Wu, 21
Library of Congress, 14
Shutterstock/Alex Garaev, 23 (back); Andrea Danti, 19 (front); Bruce Rolff, 5
    (design element); Gary Yim, cover; Jose Ignacio Soto, 28–29; Liudmila Gridina, 13 (front);
    Lukiyanova Natalia/frenta, 23 (top); Maksym Gorpenyuk, 7; modestlife, 25, 27; Paul B.
    Moore, 13 (back)
Wikipedia/Dawoud Khalil Messiha, 20

Printed in the United States of America in Stevens Point, Wisconsin.
032012   006678WZF12

TABLE OF CONTENTS

LOST CITIES AND ANCIENT WONDERS

Humans have answered many of the world's oldest questions. But are lost cities and **ancient** airplanes still waiting to be found? These top 10 ancient mysteries have yet to be solved.

ancient–belonging to a time long ago

THE GREAT PYRAMID OF GIZA

Around 80 pyramids stand in Giza, Egypt. The Great Pyramid is the largest of all. It stands 489 feet (149 meters) tall. How did the ancient Egyptians haul huge stone blocks to the top of the pyramid without modern technology?

technology—the use of science to do practical things, such as designing complex machines

THE HANGING GARDENS OF BABYLON

Babylon was an ancient city in the Middle East. People say the Hanging Gardens of Babylon looked like a mountain of plants. Trees, flowers, and bushes grew on steps built high in the air. Do the **ruins** of Babylon prove that these amazing gardens really existed?

ruins–the remains of a building or other things that have fallen down or been destroyed

JAPAN'S UNDERWATER RUINS

Ancient stones lie beneath the water off the shore of Japan. Some people think the stones are ruins from the lost **continent** of Mu. Believers claim that Mu mysteriously disappeared thousands of years ago.

continent–one of the large land masses of Earth

EGYPTIAN UNDERGROUND

10 9 8 7 6 5 4 3 2 1

In 1909 the Phoenix Gazette newspaper reported an amazing story. Explorers had found ruins of an ancient Egyptian city in the Grand Canyon! But today the remains are nowhere to be seen. Was the discovery covered up? Or was it a **hoax** to begin with?

hoax–a trick to make people believe something that is not true

THE DEATH OF KING TUT

King Tut's **mummy** was found in 1922. But it's not clear how the ancient Egyptian king died. Some experts think Tut's injuries show that he was killed. Others think King Tut died from a fall. Will his death remain a mystery?

mummy–a body that has been preserved

ATLANTIS

Legends tell of a lost island city called Atlantis in the Atlantic Ocean. The city was said to be destroyed by natural disasters in a single day. People have searched the world for the ruins. But Atlantis has never been found.

legend—a story handed down from earlier times; legends are often based on fact, but they are not entirely true

THE KING'S KNOT

According to legend, King Arthur was one of Britain's greatest leaders. But did he really exist? The King's Knot is a group of raised circles in Scotland. Some people believe it covers King Arthur's Round Table. Scientists plan to study what is beneath the King's Knot.

FACT The story goes that King Arthur's table was round so that his knights received equal respect.

ANCIENT AIRPLANES

Carvings that look like airplanes have been found in ancient ruins. American Indians have told stories about flying machines for thousands of years. Could people have built airplanes long ago?

Odd carvings were discovered at a temple in Abydos, Egypt, in 1848. At that time, people didn't know what they were. Today most people recognize them as aircraft.

THE MAYAN CALENDAR

The Mayans were ancient American Indians. They created a calendar that tracked the sun, stars, and planets. The Mayan calendar ends on December 21, 2012. What does that date stand for? Some people fear it marks an Earth-changing event.

FACT

The start date for the Mayan calendar was August 11, 3114 BC.

Mayan calendar

Mayan ruins

EASTER ISLAND

More than 500 years ago, carvers built hundreds of stone figures called Moai on Easter Island. These statues stood 13 feet (4 meters) high and weighed 14 tons (12.7 metric tons). Many of them still line the island's coast.

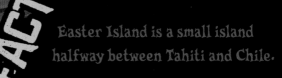

FACT

Easter Island is a small island
halfway between Tahiti and Chile.

Nobody knows why the Easter Islanders made the Moai or how they moved them. But experts might know why the people disappeared. Scientists think they used up their **natural resources**. Today only their statues are left behind.

natural resource–any substance found in nature that people use, such as soil, air, trees, coal, and oil

SOLVING THE PUZZLES

2

Scientists keep looking for clues to these puzzles. New discoveries happen every day. Maybe one day you can solve one of these top 10 unexplained ancient mysteries!

Glossary

ancient (AYN-shunt)—belonging to a time long ago

continent (KAHN-tuh-nuhnt)—one of the large land masses of Earth

hoax (HOHKS)—a trick to make people believe something that is not true

legend (LEJ-uhnd)—a story handed down from earlier times; legends are often based on fact, but they are not entirely true

mummy (MUH-mee)—a body that has been preserved

natural resource (REE-sorss)—any substance found in nature that people use, such as soil, air, trees, coal, and oil

ruins (ROO-ins)—the remains of a building or other things that have fallen down or been destroyed

technology (tek-NOL-uh-jee)—the use of science to do practical things, such as designing complex machines

Read More

Matthews, Rupert. *Ancient Mysteries.* Unexplained. Mankato, Minn.: QEB Publications, 2010.

Hawkins, John. *Atlantis and Other Lost Worlds.* Mystery Hunters. New York: PowerKids Press, 2012.

Reis, Ronald A. *Easter Island.* Lost Worlds and Mysterious Civilizations. New York: Chelsea House, 2011.

Internet Sites

FactHound offers a safe, fun way to find Internet sites related to this book. All of the sites on FactHound have been researched by our staff.

Here's all you do:

Visit *www.facthound.com*

Type in this code: 9781429684378

Super-cool stuff!

Check out projects, games and lots more at
www.capstonekids.com

Index